D1266413

Show Me
TRANSPORTATION

My First Picture Encyclopedia

by Mari Schuh

Riverhead Free Library
330 Court Street
Riverhead, New York 11901

CAPSTONE PRESS
a capstone imprint

A+ Books are published by Capstone Press,
1710 Roe Crest Drive, North Mankato, Minnesota 56003.
www.capstonepub.com

Copyright © 2013 by Capstone Press, a Capstone imprint.
All rights reserved.
No part of this publication may be reproduced in whole or in part,
or stored in a retrieval system, or transmitted in any form or by any means, electronic, mechanical,
photocopying, recording, or otherwise, without written permission of the publisher.
For information regarding permission, write to Capstone Press,
1710 Roe Crest Drive, North Mankato, Minnesota 56003.

Library of Congress Cataloging-in-Publication Data
Schuh, Mari C., 1975–
  Show me transportation : my first picture encyclopedia / by Mari Schuh.
    p. cm. — (A+. My first picture encyclopedias)
  Summary: "Defines through text and photos core terms related to
    transportation"—Provided by publisher.
  ISBN 978-1-4296-8570-2 (library binding)
  ISBN 978-1-62065-198-8 (ebook PDF)
  1. Motor vehicles—Juvenile literature. 2. Picture books for children. I. Title.
  TL147.S38 2013
  629.04′6—dc23   2012008165

Editorial Credits
Kristen Mohn, editor; Tracy Davies McCabe, designer; Svetlana Zhurkin, media researcher;
    Laura Manthe, production specialist

Photo Credits
Alamy: David L. Moore, 23 (bottom left); Dreamstime: Dmitry Mizintsev, 10 (bottom), Frogtravel, 18 (top left), Georgii Dolgykh, 4 (top), Joseph Gough, 19 (top left), Ltreat, 19 (bottom right), Mashe, 16 (top), Mlan61, 23 (bottom right), Photocell, 19 (bottom left), Pierdelune, 25 (middle left), Victoria Whitehead, 19 (top right); Getty Images: Allsport/David Taylor, 10 (top left); iStockphotos: Mike Clarke, 19 (middle), Sun Chan, 17 (bottom left), sundown001, 20 (top); NASA, 11 (bottom), 30, 31 (middle and bottom), JPL, 30 (top); Newscom: Agence France Presse/Neil Munns, 10 (top right), EPN/FeatureChina/EyePress, 21 (bottom right); Shutterstock: Alaettin Yildirim, 16 (bottom right), Alex Mit, 13 (middle right), Anastasija Popova, 7 (middle right), Andresr, 5 (bottom right), Angela Jones (tire tracks), cover and throughout, Angelo Gilardelli, 22, B. Stefanov, 23 (middle), bhathaway, back cover (right), Brad Sauter, 20 (bottom left), Brian Upton (jetliner), cover, 1, Bufflerump, 5 (bottom left), Christopher Halloran, 11 (top left), creativedoxfoto, 7 (top right), Darren Brode, 8 (bottom right), Dhoxax, 25 (top left), Dmitry Kalinovsky, 17 (top), E.G.Pors, 6 (top left), Elena Elisseeva, 9 (bottom left), Elnur (torn paper), cover, 1, Eric Broder Van Dyke, 9 (top right), fotohunter, 21 (bottom left), Goce Risteski, 6 (bottom right), 13 (bottom left), greatpapa, 16 (bottom left), GSK, back cover (left), 18 (bottom), GTibbetts, 17 (bottom right), Hung Chung Chih, 9 (bottom right), Ilja Mašík, 7 (top left), Jeff Schultes, 25 (middle right), JEO, 8 (top right), Juan Camilo Bernal, 8 (bottom left), Karl R. Martin, 14 (bottom), lightpoet, 13 (top), Luminis, 27 (top), Lusoimages, 17 (middle), Margo Harrison, 4 (bottom), 23 (top left), Markus Gann, 31 (star background), Mecc, 9 (top left), nadirco, 25 (top right), Nailia Schwarz, 27 (bottom), Oleg Zabielin, 25 (bottom), Paul Vinten, 6 (bottom left), PixAchi, 8 (top left), Pres Panayotov (cargo ship), cover, Rafael Ramirez Lee, 6 (top right), Rihardzz, 5 (top left), 23 (top right), Rob Wilson, cover (semitruck), 12, 14 (top), 15, 18 (top right), Robert Pernell, 5 (middle), robophobic, 9 (middle right), rorem, 20 (bottom right), Rudy Balasko, 13 (bottom right), Sergios, 11 (top right), Simon Krzic, 24 (bottom), smart.art, 24 (top), Sony Ho, 13 (middle left), StudioSmart, 26, Supertrooper, 7 (bottom), Tatiana Makotra, 21 (top), Thomas Bethge, 9 (middle left), Tungphoto, cover (hot air balloon), Tupungato, 5 (top right), Walter G. Arce, 11 (middle right), Wansfordphoto, 7 (middle left), ypkim (helicopter), cover; U.S. Air Force, 11 (middle left), Staff Sgt. M. Erick Reynolds, 29 (top right), Staff Sgt. Shane A. Cuomo, 29 (bottom right); U.S. Army: Sgt. 1st Class Sandra Watkins-Keough, 29 (bottom left); U.S. Navy: Chief Mass Communication Specialist John Lill, 28 (top left), Lockheed Martin Corp., 29 (top left), Mass Communication Specialist 2nd Class Casey H. Kyhl, 28 (top right), Mass Communication Specialist 3rd Class Travis K. Mendoza, 29 (middle), Mass Communication Specialist Seaman John Grandin, 28 (bottom)

Note to Parents, Teachers, and Librarians
My First Picture Encyclopedias provide an early introduction to reference materials for young children. These accessible, visual encyclopedias support literacy development by building subject-specific vocabularies and research skills. Stimulating format, inviting content, and phonetic aids assist and encourage young readers.

The author dedicates this book to Jacob Caruso of Kenosha, Wisconsin, who quietly listens for whistles of faraway choo-choo cars.

Printed in the United States of America in North Mankato, Minnesota.

042012   006682CGF12

Table of Contents

On the Move

Walking is one way to get from place to place. But when the places are far apart, it's time to travel in other ways—by land, water, or air.

ON LAND

car

the first gas-powered cars were invented in France and Germany in the 1880s; early models were called "horseless carriages"

motorcycle

a vehicle with two wheels and an engine, built for one or two people

tractor

a large farm vehicle with big tires used to pull other farm machines or equipment

streetcar

a vehicle that looks like a bus but that runs on rails in the street; streetcars, or trolleys, usually have electric motors

semitruck

a large truck that has 10 or more wheels and is used to transport goods

taxi

a car driven by someone who is hired to drive people where they want to go; many taxis are bright yellow

bus

buses are a common form of public transportation; some buses in England have two levels, and lots of people ride them to go sightseeing

ON THE WATER

cruise ship

a very large ship that carries people to places around the world; the world's biggest cruise ship, *Allure of the Seas*, holds more than 8,000 people and is like a floating city

cargo ship

a ship that carries goods across the ocean; cargo ships carry their cargo in large, metal shipping containers

yacht

(YAWT)—a kind of sailing powerboat used for racing and for relaxing

personal watercraft

a small machine that zips across lakes and bounces over waves; riders use handlebars to steer

BY AIR

jetliner

a large plane with a wide body that can carry a few hundred people; a Boeing 747 jetliner is so big, 45 cars could fit on its wings

hot air balloon

an aircraft made of a very large bag or balloon filled with hot air or gas that causes it to float; people ride in a basket that hangs below the balloon

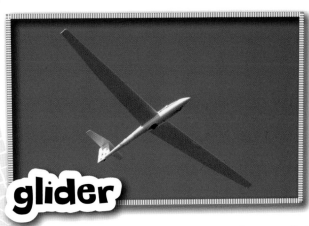

glider

an airplane without an engine; gliders are started by launching from high places or they can be towed and released from an airplane in flight

stunt plane

these small planes spin, dive, and loop in the air as tricks for people to watch

helicopter

helicopters have spinning blades that lift the aircraft straight up into the air

Power Sources

Long ago people used their muscles or the help of animals to move things. But today people use different energy sources to power vehicles.

engine

(EN-juhn)—engines are machines that turn energy into force and motion; many fast cars have their engines in the middle or back of the car, which lets power go straight to the back wheels for more speed

fuel

a source of energy used to move vehicles; types of fuel include diesel, gasoline, and ethanol, which is made from corn or other crops

electric vehicle

some cars are powered by an electric motor; electric cars get energy from large batteries that can be recharged

hybrid vehicle

a vehicle that runs partly on gas and partly on electricity

steam

a steam engine uses water and wood, coal, or oil to work; water is heated to make steam, which makes energy to move the engine's parts

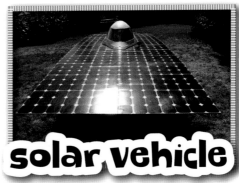

solar vehicle

a vehicle that gets power from the sun's energy; most solar vehicles are still being tested

blimp

a round airship with gas inside that makes it float; blimps are often used for sightseeing and for advertising

sailboat

a boat that is pushed by the wind, which is caught in huge canvas sails; most sailboats also have a small motor

People Power

People can still get from place to place using their own muscle power. Time to move your arms and legs!

canoe (kuh-NEW)—a small, narrow, open boat that holds a few people and is rowed by oars

rickshaw—a vehicle that looks like a chair and is powered by a person walking or on a bicycle; rickshaws take passengers for short rides

rickshaw

canoe

Built for Speed

Ever since the first vehicles were built, people have been looking for ways to go faster and faster. How fast will we go? Hang on tight!

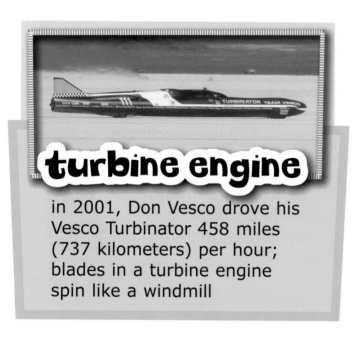

turbine engine

in 2001, Don Vesco drove his Vesco Turbinator 458 miles (737 kilometers) per hour; blades in a turbine engine spin like a windmill

jet engine

an engine creates power from a stream of gases under pressure; in 1997, the Thrust SSC car used jet engines and special wheels to speed up to 771 miles (1,241 km) per hour

high-speed train

high-speed trains in some countries in Europe and Asia can reach speeds of more than 200 miles (322 km) per hour

drag racing

in drag racing, two cars race on a straight course; Top Fuel drag racing cars can speed from 0 to 100 miles (0 to 161 km) per hour in less than one second

speedboat

a boat people drive for fun and in races; the world speedboat record is 317 miles (510 km) per hour

X-15 Aircraft

the rocket-powered X-15 flew 4,520 miles (7,274 km) per hour; it was used for research

Daytona 500

a race where cars cruise around an oval track 200 times; in 2011, Trevor Bayne won the Daytona 500 with an average speed of 130 miles (209 km) per hour

space shuttle

space shuttles carried astronauts to space for 30 years; they sped upward at 17,500 miles (28,000 km) per hour to escape Earth's gravity

On the Road: Cars

It takes hundreds and hundreds of parts of all shapes and sizes working together to make a car go. Buckle up, and take a ride!

bumper
heavy metal or plastic bumpers on the fronts and backs of cars protect them during an accident

headlight
lights on the front of a car help the driver to see clearly and help others see the car in the dark

tire
a rubber ring around a car's wheel; tires help slow the car down when the driver pushes on the brakes

seat belt

a strap that holds a person safely in a car; in most of the United States and Canada, laws make people wear seat belts to stay safe

steering wheel

the wheel inside a car used to control where the car goes; in some countries, cars have the steering wheel on the right side instead of the left, and cars drive on the opposite side of the road

air bag

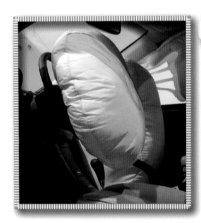

a bag inside a car that fills with air to keep people safe during a car crash; after a crash, air bags fill up in less than 1 second

axle

(AK-suhl)—a rod in the middle of a wheel; wheels turn on axles

transmission

(trans-MISH-uhn)—a piece of equipment that carries power from the engine to the wheels and allows the engine to run at a constant speed; the transmission is used to go from no speed to highway speed

chassis

(CHASS-ee)—a car's metal frame, like the skeleton of the vehicle

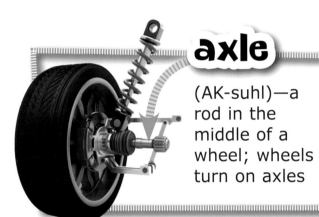

On the Road: Trucks

Ever wonder how your food or favorite sneakers reach the stores? They're brought in by trucks rumbling in from across town, across the state, and even across the country. Here are some cool truck parts.

tanker

a long truck with a big tank to carry liquid goods, such as milk, syrup, gas, oil, water, or chemicals

trailer

a large metal box towed behind the cab where goods are carried; when a truck is driving without the trailer, it's called "bobtailing"

exhuast pipe

(eg-SAWST)—a pipe that carries burned gases from the engine to the outside air; on semis, exhaust pipes usually run up the sides of the cab like chimneys

air deflector

(dih-FLEKT-ur)—a rounded part on the top of the cab that helps air move smoothly over the truck so it can move faster

sideview mirror

mirrors on both sides of the cab allow the driver to see what's coming behind; these mirrors are heated to keep ice from forming on them in cold weather

cab

the front part of the truck with the controls and the driver's seat; some cabs have sleeping areas for drivers to use during rest stops

fuel tank

fuel for the engine is held in tanks behind or under the cab

Time to Build:
Construction Vehicles

Vehicles do more than just get people from place to place. Construction vehicles help workers build long, flat roads and tall, sleek buildings.

dump truck

a truck with a large container that can hold and dump dirt and rocks; giant dump trucks used for mining are about as long as a humpback whale and taller than a two-story building!

bulldozer

a vehicle that has a strong blade on the front to move dirt and rocks

forklift

a small truck with two large prongs on the front; the "fork" is positioned so it fits under something that needs to be moved or lifted

backhoe

a vehicle used for digging holes or filling trenches with dirt; legs on the front of the backhoe keep the machine still

concrete mixer

a truck with a large egg-shaped container that mixes and pours concrete; the container spins to mix the concrete

On the Streets

There are many other hard-working vehicles with important jobs to do!

garbage truck—a truck that takes garbage to the dump; garbage trucks smash garbage bags to make room for more; many garbage trucks have special arms that pick up and empty trash cans

snowplow—a big vehicle with a plow on the front that clears snow off roads

snowplow

garbage truck

Emergency Vehicles

When people need help, a variety of emergency vehicles leap into action to bring them to safety. Listen for the sirens as these vehicles race to help!

police car

police cars flash their lights and race to the scene of a crime or accident; one of fastest police cars in the world can go 225 miles (362 km) per hour

ambulance

a vehicle with a large rear passenger area designed to carry sick or hurt people to the hospital

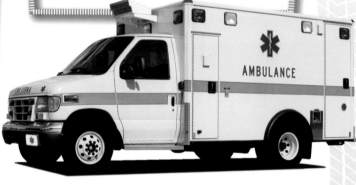

fire truck

a big truck that races to a fire and helps put it out; fire trucks carry firefighters, water, ladders, and equipment

rescue boat

a boat used by the U.S. Coast Guard and others to rescue people in trouble in the water

rescue helicopter

helicopters can be used to rescue people in places other vehicles can't reach

tow truck

a strong truck that moves broken or damaged vehicles

air tanker

a special plane that is filled with water and chemicals to put out fires

fire boat

fire boats use the water they are floating on to fight fires on ships or along shore

On the Tracks: Trains

Trains can carry products or people long distances in a short amount of time. On some trains, people can sleep and eat as they travel across the country. All aboard!

locomotive
a powerful machine that pulls a train

freight
trains carry freight such as coal, grain, sugar, sand, wood, and vegetables

subway
a kind of train that cruises under city streets through tunnels

monorail

a train that moves on one rail instead of two; some monorail trains travel on tracks built high above the ground, while others run at street level or underground

tracks

rails on the ground that a train travels on; tracks take trains over land, across bridges, and through tunnels

maglev

a high-speed maglev train doesn't have wheels—it quietly floats above a special track using strong magnets

Two-Wheel Transportation: Bikes and Motorbikes

The first bicycles were different from today's bikes. Early bikes were made of wood! Now bikes are built for speed and comfort. Some even have small motors for racing on curvy dirt roads.

mountain bike

a strong bike with flat handlebars, wide tires, and many speeds for riding on rough, bumpy trails and hills

gear

the higher gears on a bike make the bike go faster but harder to pedal; the lower gears on a bike make the bike go slower but easier to pedal

brake

the brake makes a bike stop; brake types include coaster, rod, caliper, drum, and disk

wheel

a bike wheel is made up of an outer rim, a center hub, and spokes that go from the hub to the rim

pocket bike

a mini motorcycle used for racing and transportation; pocket bikes are tiny, but they can reach speeds of 47 miles (76 km) per hour

BMX bike

a small bike used for racing, jumping, and doing stunts; BMX stands for bicycle motocross

motocross bike

a bike with a small motor made to zoom around on bumpy dirt tracks; motocross bikes have tires that grip the track

recumbent bike

(rih-KUM-bent)—riders sit back while pedaling a recumbent bike

scooter

a small motorized vehicle with two wheels used for riding around town

23

Set Sail: Boats and Ships

People use boats and ships to sail for fun and to transport goods. Boats come in all different sizes and shapes to fit their jobs out on the water.

barge

a boat with a flat bottom that carries heavy items such as steel, wood, and grain along rivers

tugboat

small, strong boats that pull or push big ships and barges in and out of harbors

river raft

a strong raft filled with air used to travel on rough waters; people use paddles to steer the raft

hydrofoil

a fast boat that rises above the water's surface with underwater wings called foils to make it zip across the water

gondola

(GAWN-duh-luh)—tourists ride in flat-bottomed gondolas in Venice, Italy; a person called a gondolier stands in the gondola and rows the boat with a long oar

ferry

a boat that takes people and cars on short trips across rivers and lakes; many people who live near water ride ferries to work

oil tanker

oil tankers are ships that carry oil all around the world; some tankers can carry 2 million barrels of oil

kayak

a small, narrow boat that is mostly covered; a person uses a paddle to move the kayak while they face forward with their legs inside the kayak

Up, Up, and Away: Flying Vehicles

Airplanes are heavier than air, so how do they fly? Many hard-working parts keep these big machines high in the sky!

cockpit
the area where the pilots sit to fly the plane; cockpits are filled with instruments and controls

throttle
the lever that controls the power in the engine

yoke
the handles that pilots use to control different parts on the airplane

aileron and flap

(AY-luh-rahn)—hinged parts of a wing that the pilot moves to turn or slow down the airplane

fuselage

(FYOO-suh-lahzh)—the tube-shaped body of the aircraft that holds all of the airplane's pieces together; some airplanes carry fuel in the fuselage

rudder

the rudder controls the plane's movement from side to side

landing gear

tires and shock absorbers that fold out of the plane before landing

propeller

spinning blades on the front of an airplane that move the aircraft through the air; propellers are powered by an engine and spin around like a fan

27

Military Vehicles

All sorts of big and strong vehicles help the military carry troops and fight enemies by land, sea, and air.

submarine

(SUHB-muh-reen) submarines are long, thin ships that move underwater; big submarines can carry nearly 150 people

amphibious vehicle

(am-FIH-bee-uhs)—amphibious vehicles are able to travel on both land and water; some go as fast as 40 miles (64 km) per hour on land

destroyer

a long, fast warship with weapons that are used to keep other ships safe; destroyers are longer than a football field

bomber

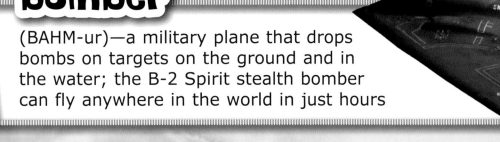

(BAHM-ur)—a military plane that drops bombs on targets on the ground and in the water; the B-2 Spirit stealth bomber can fly anywhere in the world in just hours

fighter plane

a jet used by the military; fighter jets refuel in the air with help from a tanker aircraft

aircraft carrier

a ship with a big flat deck where planes take off and land; aircraft carriers are runways in the ocean and can hold more than 60 aircraft

Humvee

a strong military truck; Humvees have an air tube called an engine snorkel that lets their engines run underwater

tank

a vehicle that moves on two tracks and is covered in armor

Blast Off: Space Vehicles

3, 2, 1, blast off! Spacecraft zoom through space to find out more about our universe. Maybe you'll ride in one someday!

Orion

(o-RYE-uhn)— a spacecraft that will take astronauts into deep space and then bring them back to Earth; *Orion* may also take supplies and crews to the *International Space Station*

rocket

a long vehicle that is powerful enough to launch people and objects into space

launch pad

(LAWNCH)—the area where a rocket takes off

orbit

to travel in space around a planet or other object

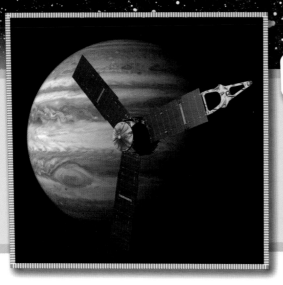

probe

a spacecraft with tools that gather information about planets and space; probes have explored all the planets in our solar system

LRO

LRO stands for the *Lunar Reconnaissance Orbiter*; it is a spacecraft that flies around the moon, taking photos and gathering information

Soyuz

a Russian spacecraft that takes astronauts to the *International Space Station* and back; a trip to the space station takes two days

rover

a vehicle that explores the surface of the moon and the planet Mars; some rovers take pictures; someday rovers that look like monster trucks might drive on Mars

Read More

Barraclough, Sue. *On the Move.* Me and My World. New York: Alphabet Soup/Windmill Books, 2009.

Demarest, Chris L. *All Aboard!: A Traveling Alphabet.* New York: Margaret K. McElderry Books, 2008.

Ipcizade, Catherine. *H Is for Honk! A Transportation Alphabet.* Alphabet Fun. Mankato, Minn.: Capstone Press, 2011.

Tourville, Amanda Doering. *Transportation in the City.* My Community. Mankato, Minn.: Capstone Press, 2011.

Internet Sites

FactHound offers a safe, fun way to find Internet sites related to this book. All of the sites on FactHound have been researched by our staff.

Here's all you do:

Visit *www.facthound.com*

Type in this code: 9781429685702

Check out projects, games and lots more at
www.capstonekids.com